Who is Madam Zucchini?

Doris Voss Dasenbrock (aka Madam Zucchini) spent many hours in the kitchen baking with her son when he was young. One of their favorite recipes was Aunt Vicki's Zucchini Bread. He loved to be in the kitchen to "help mix it." He started calling her Madam Zucchini whenever they would bake, no matter what they were making. Still she is called Madam Zucchini when baking or cooking in the kitchen. You can find the family favorite Zucchini Bread recipe on her web site:

www.madamzucchini.com

I0173394

Forward

This is a poem story about Madam Zucchini and The Gardener. They get multiple surprises when they discover what is happening in Madam Zucchini's *Garden of Surprises* during the evening hours. The Gardener receives a BirdCam™ for Christmas and the nocturnal Night Marauder adventure begins. Just how many Night Marauders are there? They seek the answer to this and other questions. The story develops into an investigation of what is happening at night. Madam Zucchini and The Gardener have had no clue about their visitors until the Christmas gift becomes the means for discovery!

This poem story is a nature and animal lover's delight. It captures the essence of wilderness inside a well-populated suburban community. The housing lots are modest, large enough to attract only birds and unleashed dogs and stray cats. Yet, here Madam Zucchini and The Gardener find unusual guests—hence they named their garden, *The Garden of Surprises*.

The photographs included in the story are the actual photographs taken by The Gardener with the BirdCam™ camera. They showed the nocturnal activities of the critters that came to the patio for food.

The vocabulary of the poem story is suitable for grade 6 and above. Older readers may also find the story amusing because it is written in a fun, witty and imaginative manner. Some words may need explanations and/or a dictionary. The structure of the poem is loose and non-conforming. It is an enjoyable read, filled with a growing anticipation of not knowing what to expect next.

This poem story should provoke a serious discussion as to why the animals come to Madam Zucchini's patio. After the poem story ends, there is an ecological epilogue as to the plight of our wild animal populations when land development pushes them out of their natural habitats. Their survival is in question once their environment dramatically changes with the suburban sprawl. It poses the question, should the animals be fed or not?

The Night Marauder

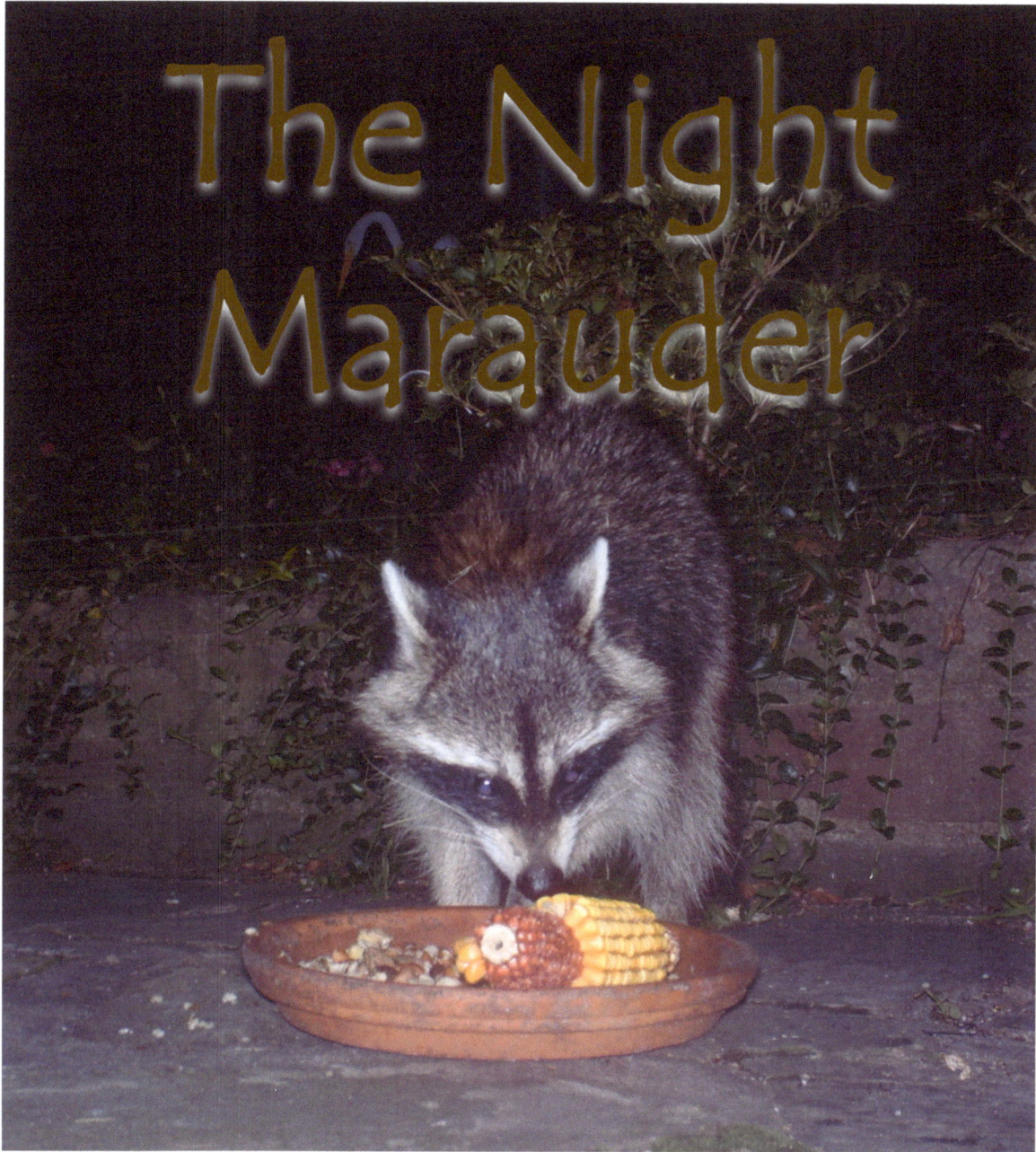

Written by
Doris Voss Dasenbrock

Early spring in the *The Garden of Surprises*

The Night Marauder

Madam Zucchini was sitting on the patio, in her favorite chair, deep in thought.
She tried to organize her ideas but they wouldn't line up as she thought they ought.

A multitude of images inside her head, went 'round and 'round.
Try as she might, in her brain there was no logic or strategy yet to be found.
The Gardener had told her, "Something is causing an open path on the ground."

The trail in the liriopes "that grew compact and broader."

Perhaps they could identify the *mysterious* culprit when it makes its appearance uttering a sound.
Could it be a stray dog that had escaped from the neighborhood or the nearby dog pound?

A lesson to this nocturnal destructive visitor needed to be taught.
Somehow this **Night Marauder,** that The Gardener had spoken of, had to
        be caught.
A definite answer to this conundrum, while not urgent, was desperately sought.
If left unchecked, much of The Gardener's hard work will have been for naught.
Exposing the critter would not be easy; it could be with potential
        disasters fraught.

T his nighttime visitor, they now referred to as the *mysterious*
        Night Marauder.
The small path it created, in time, was a trail that grew compact and broader.
There were tracks and disruption near the house foundation and around the
        pond's edge.
There were plants uprooted next to the water where the liriopes hung over a
        ledge.

" N othing will re-grow there. Heaven knows I've tried," The Gardener
        lamented.
"It is as if the dirt along the pathway had been recently cemented."
This area of ruined plants and packed dirt any good gardener would have
        resented.

" S omething is destroying *anything* that tries there to sprout and grow.
What creature is doing it," The Gardener stated, "I just have to know. It gets
trampled on and beaten down, causing an empty spot in the border plant row."
He mumbled, "I don't think it's that big bull frog hopping up from the pond
        below.
It'll take several years for new plants to regenerate and fill in the empty space,
        from experience, this I know.
You can't just toss out the seeds on compact earth and expect them to grow."
The Gardener chuckled, "The bright side is that at least bare ground I won't
        have to mow."

"I don't think it's that big bull frog hopping up from the pond below."

"If I sit up all-night, I might catch it in the act," The Gardener stated and
    added, "I think that could work."
But was it worth the loss of sleep? Being tired the next day, many of his labors
    he'd have to shirk.
He felt he *just had to catch the villain* as it trundled about in the garden,
    blissfully unaware.
The critter, he supposed, would amble along here and there without a worry
    or a care.

But to sit up all night just to find out, seemed to him to be a bit too extreme.
Still, to capture the thief in the act, wasn't to him, as crazy as to others it
    might seem.

Surely, another surveillance method he should be able to devise.

After all, he was an acknowledged experienced gardener, being in these matters, very wise.

But so far he came up empty-handed, despite all his attempts and numerous tries.

What he really needed in *The Garden of Surprises* were several helpful well-placed spies.

He wondered how long it would be before some modicum of success he would realize.

Every night The Gardener put out food so the birds could eat early the next morn.

Sometimes it was nuts and a bit of bread that he had broken apart and carefully torn.

Often, he would additionally put out a cob of dried yellow field corn.

"The early bird gets the worm" was an adage he remembered; it was well worn.

He used to inwardly scoff at that old saying almost to the point of visible scorn.

For he realized that sage adage was in use long before *he* was born.

He knew the birds were early risers; he heard their noisy chatter and singing at daybreak.
It woke him up far too early, long before he wanted to rise and stay awake.

He didn't anticipate, what was to come by putting food out for the birds the night before.
He couldn't know in advance what for him was really in store.
How could he suspect something else would sneak stealthily into *the garden* to intrude?
YET, some other creature DARED to nocturnally slip into *the garden* and scarf up the birds' food.

He didn't foresee that by morning there would be absolutely nothing left for the birds to eat.
Who would guess another creature would fill up on what was supposed to be the birds' treat?

He now suspected that uprooted plants and missing bird food were the earmarks of a **Night Marauder**.
The evidence was there, it was plain to see-it could not be broader.

A large terra cotta-colored flowerpot liner is where the food was placed overnight in wait.
But now, he reasoned, "I will have to use this food for the **Night Marauder's** bait.
You and I, *mysterious* **Night Marauder**, have a pending, as yet unspecified date."

The long days lingered on, then finally, the long, humid, hot summer turned cool in the fall.
The autumn days' hours of sunlight grew short; the afternoons' purple shadows grew tall.
One day, Madam Zucchini and The Gardener decided they had to go to the shopping mall.

Their mission was to replenish the birdseed; so they were off to their nearby favorite bird supply store.
Having gotten a late start, they were relieved to see an **"OPEN"** sign on the front door.

Once inside the shop, they spent a good deal of time browsing, just looking around.
Then **voila!** A possible answer to their perplexing quest, they both instantly found.

There displayed on the wall, and in boxes on the floor, were cameras that took photos of things that move.
Perhaps with such a camera, the **Night Marauder's** identity, a photo would prove!

The camera was activated by a motion-sensor; it could photograph
movement by night or day.
"With this device," said The Gardener, "I can finally prove what creature has
been stealing the food away."

Madam Zucchini agreed, "The camera will capture the **Night Marauder**
eating off the birds' food plate.
You then wouldn't feel compelled to have to stay up all night keeping watch
until very late."

BUT...she wondered should they buy it now or later? That was the
question that caused the big debate.
They decided to do camera research first, so the camera purchase would just
have to wait.

Madam Zucchini and The Gardener left the bird store, with their packaged
birdseed in hand.
The camera was very expensive; but would it really work for what they
had hoped for and planned?

The debate lasted long after Halloween, Thanksgiving, and even into the
middle of the Christmas season.
Why had they not purchased the camera? Well, doubt that it would work and
possibly wasting money was the reason.

But on December 25th, under the Christmas tree, sat a box pushed far to
the back.
The Gardener wondered whom it was meant for, because a tag it did lack.

Surprise!

It was a gift for The Gardener; he opened it slowly enjoying the moment; he wanted it to last.

The Gardener relished the paper and box unfolding; unlike anxious children who opened their gifts much too fast.

Inside the box he found *that an action sensing camera was his gift; 'twas a present from his son.*

This gift was *his answer;* he grinned from ear to ear; with this gift he felt a new adventure had begun.

He would set the camera up in *The Garden of Surprises;* he wanted to do it that very night.

He could hardly wait to see what was really going on out there, out of everyone's sight.

He would be able to see the creature that nocturnally marauded in the dark.
Soon he'd know which one had visited *the garden* and left its mark.

He sat quietly reflecting on which one the critter most likely would be.
An opossum, raccoon, groundhog, fox, deer, skunk, any or all of these he
       might see.

All had been seen at least one time in and around the neighborhood before.
He could hardly contain his explosion of thoughts trying to project what for
       them was in store.

But alas, bad weather set in; it was nasty and slushy, like a mixture of slurry.
There was a cold frigid air mass from Canada with a wind that blew with gale-
       like fury.
Along with the blustery cold air came deep drifting snow, dropped in a
       whirlwind of quick blinding flakes in a flurry.

The Gardener was disappointed that by the weather he was a captive held
       inside.
That this wasn't the time to mount the camera and test it, he couldn't abide.
The very next day, icy and wintry cold as it was, he tried. He really tried.
The frosty wind whipped around him and made him all teary and watery-eyed.

Frost bit into his face, ice stuck to his mustache; his cheeks were pelted with
       icy sharp crystals that stung.
He now realized there was no hope to use the camera; besides many animals
       had burrowed in for a hard winter's run.
It would be a long time before they felt the warmth and glow of the orbiting
       earth back to summer's sun.

The months of winter stayed with a vengeful force; bad weather lashed out with a full gale.

It was so blustery that the deep drifting snows would have hidden the Night Marauder's trail.

This Arctic blast, "the Canada Clipper," made even the strongest people feel weak and frail.

Each day The Gardener looked out of the greenhouse shed hoping warm temps would prevail.

But each ensuing day, winter's cold breath swooshed down ferociously without fail.

Madam Zucchini's garden looked like a magical gleaming fairyland so pure, so white.
The only problem was that this lovely picture scene should have been long gone; it wasn't right!
Yet neither Madam Zucchini nor The Gardener could deny the beauty of the sight.

The sunlight on the glistening scene made changing patterns through the trees on the snow.
Seeing the thick blanket of white, it was hard to imagine that under this covered sight, vegetation would again grow.
But consulting the pages of *The Farmer's Almanac* would, in black and white, show it to be so.
Spring would be coming around again, as in years past, albeit, much too slow.
The Gardener tried to comfort himself again with the idea that at least, there was no grass to mow.

Yet, mowing aside, he looked forward to when time advanced and the
        temperatures would rise;
Then instead of dark gray clouds there would be white wispy mares' tails in
        pure blue skies.

He wanted to put an end to this austere two-tone frozen tundra-like view.
It was past time for a dramatic change; he wanted a vibrant emerald green
        scene, totally new.
He often looked out the patio window at the many bird feeders brimming
        with seeds.
At least if he couldn't work outside, he could meet the critters' winter
        food needs.

The snow was piled high upon the patio furniture almost obscuring it
    from sight.
It was winter's law that all growth activity was frozen in time, until the passage
    of time was right.
This total blanket coverage of pure white and colorlessness seemed like
    nature's blight.
Until it melted he would keep a path open, tossing out seeds on the snow
    for the birds' and squirrels' delight.

This deep shroud of blanketed snow was both beautiful and yet, almost
    depressing to see.
It meant, if the groundhog, Punxsutawney Phil, sees his shadow, 6 weeks of
    more winter weather there would be.

Waiting for winter to leave was such a strain; he longed to feel spring's fresh smelling rain.
The Gardener kept busy; he was not idle during the long harsh winter; he eagerly planned his new garden; he couldn't abstain.

He thumbed through many garden catalogues looking for new plant varieties and hybrids to try.
Although not all had survived, he decided his favorites he'd renew even if they were a risky buy that might in the future die.

He reviewed his past butterfly attracting preferences that had been choices of great satisfaction.
Although other plants he selected had passable results, he sometimes got a startling reaction.

Flowers that should have been four feet tall had surpassed their limit and grew seven feet high and had to be propped up against the house wall.
The Gardener was disappointed; he had wanted and planned for them to be quite small.

He recalled that some perennials had refused to return in the spring as the nursery proclaimed they would.
This caused The Gardener consternation because they were supposed to come up yearly like he expected they should.

His frustration did not bring the plants back; it wasted his time, and drained his good will.
But each and every year enthusiasm returned, and as spring drew near, he could hardly sit still.

His tools had long ago been cleaned, sharpened and oiled ready for the garden work to begin.
They were stored neatly near a fertilizer bin.
Had he not had them ready to use, for The Gardener, would have been not quite, but almost, a sin.

Finally, **finally**, after a long hard winter came the spring, along with pouring drenching rains too.
Of yard work there were so few dry days and there was so much work that he had yet to do.
Discovering varmints lost priority; there was no time to set up the camera, test it, adjust it, and retest it anew.

That would have to wait until after the pruning and planting took place.
The spring's annual flowers needed to be planted to give the garden a look of elegance and grace.

The tulip bulbs, long ago, had been a gourmet delicacy devoured by voles and/or moles.
All over the yard there had been signs of their presence – their tunnels and holes.

But by the beginning of summer, all of the garden planting had finally come
to an end.
Animals had come out of their winter burrows; they had lost fat in hibernation;
they all had an empty stomach to mend.
There was now time to fiddle with the camera, to see what pictures it would
send.

The Gardener set up the camera on a tripod to hold it tight.
He hoped the fabled Night Marauder would soon come into his sight.
Eureka! When he downloaded the photos into his computer, the images
revealed the marauder in the night.
For the Night Marauder was a raccoon that was eating to his heart's delight.

That photo showed the black masked burglar; he was a varmint with rings
        on his tail; he wore a wet, soggy brown coat of fur.
He had been suspected as "an animal of interest," but the Gardener, from the
        photo, couldn't be sure if it was a "him or her."

There had been visitations by many creatures to *The Garden of Surprises*
        long before.
The Garden of Surprises was named because of the visitations by a variety of
        creatures that had come to the patio door.

Unfortunately, there was only one photo of the varmint raccoon before the
        critter was perhaps shocked by the camera's sudden flash.
The Gardener presumed the critter took off frightened by the bright light,
        probably in a hurried mad dash.

Now finally Madam Zucchini and The Gardener had photographic proof
        of **The Marauder** at the patio site.
They had caught him with a photo eating away at the birds' food in the
        middle of the night.

Having a photograph, as evidence should have been enough, but was it?
What if there were other critters out there yet still unseen?
What if there were others cavorting about in *the garden* green?

Could there be more than one raccoon, eating all the food?
"It is worth investigating," The Gardener said, "I want to know with certitude."

The Gardener decided more pictures would be beneficial and helpful to see.
Perhaps there was a pair of raccoons, or even a family of three.
So he continued to set up his camera to see what else there could be.

He set it in front of the house where there had been evidence in the dirt.
The soil had been disturbed so he wondered what out there did lurk.

The next day he checked his camera and found no photos were taken.
He muttered, "Surely there was something there, but I guess I was mistaken."

But since there were no photos taken at all, he had to find out all he could.
Why had the camera failed to operate correctly and take photos as it should?

Despite no new photos was it still functioning properly? An investigation
        needed to be made.
Had rain gotten inside or was the problem just dirt or dust or perhaps a
        grass blade?

He carefully opened the box and checked the camera inside and out.
There was nothing to indicate a malfunction or a reason its workings to doubt.

"Maybe if I change a few settings, the time between shots, could be the
        malfunctioning clue," he to himself said.
So he made adjustments for the very next night when he put out the bird
        camera near a flowerbed.

He decided to put the camera near where it had been in a similarly close spot.
But he set it lower to get a different view of any new animal shot.
When he checked the camera he was totally surprised at the photo he
actually he got.

There was a photo showing **TWO RACCOONS!** Two raccoons had come to
the patio to eat!
At around four o'clock in the morning, they had been there voraciously eating
the birds' treat.

Madam Zucchini viewed the pictures the next day and said, "This is a great surprise."
She continued. "I did not know there was one, now I see there were TWO before my eyes."
A frown crossed her brow. "Could there be even more?" she wondered aloud.
Then she said, "Just how many raccoons belong to this emerging crowd?"

The Gardener responded, "If we have more raccoons running about rampant, are they perhaps with rabies infected?
We had better continue feeding them until their numbers with certainty we've detected.
There could be a whole family around us, if those two are a mating pair, that wouldn't be unsuspected."

"But they really are so cute with their ringed tails and little bandito masks," she remarked.
Then she added, "I think just inside our house by the patio window we should ourselves be parked."
That comment in the mind of The Gardener caused an idea to have sparked.

"Yes, later at night we should plan to watch them to see just what they do," he confirmed.
"Yes, that's a really great idea," with hands clapped in enthusiasm, that plan he reaffirmed.

Madam Zucchini added, "Then we can maybe tell from which direction they came.
Or in which direction when they leave, do they run, is it the same?"

They determined that very night they would set out more food as bait.
They also decided they would "lie in wait," by sitting at the patio window
starting in the evening from eight.

It was close to eleven o'clock before they sighted another surprise.
There were now **THREE RACCOONS** out there before their very eyes!

They had wondered if a family of three there could be.
They never really expected them on their patio to see.

The camera was flashing on and off quite often with so many bodies
          moving around.
The photo review the next day showed the raccoons had been playfully rolling
          on the ground.
For the pair looking at the photos sheer excitement did abound.

Who knew or could have thought that *the garden* had these visitors at night?
Three raccoons in the middle of a well-populated suburban area didn't seem right.

Without the bird camera Madam Zucchini and The Gardener never this would
          have guessed.
The thought of **THREE RACCOONS** left both of them more than a little distressed.

Were they like mice or rabbits that kept reproducing large numbers of babies?
If so, there would be more chances of humans getting raccoon bites which often
          caused rabies.

"Oh NO, NO!" Madam Zucchini did not like to think of
          something so disagreeable.
Like it or not, that is just what to Madam Zucchini was clearly foreseeable.

The pair felt committed to keep watching each and every night.
They had to try to determine if there were even more raccoons within sight.

The nightly spying ritual had taken a lot of time but had proven to be
          enjoyable entertainment.
They laughed, while watching the raccoons playing and eating and rolling around
          without containment.

All of a sudden one night, **ANOTHER RACCOON** appeared. Now there were **FOUR**.
"Four," Madam Zucchini cried out, four raccoons outside my door!
Surely this has to be all of them, I truly hope there aren't any more!

But as she watched them, she had to laugh, they were so comical, so energetic, and so cute.
They were gobbling up everything except they didn't seem to like some of the pieces of fruit.

The night watch became so enjoyable the two sat by the window waiting for
        the animals to return.
They tried to tell the creatures apart, to see if distinctive markings on them
        they could learn.
But unfortunately, with the low light, in the dark of night, many differences,
        they couldn't discern.

They *did* notice a difference in their sizes; perhaps they started bulking up for
        the winter season.
Or, perhaps sizes varied because of their relative ages to each other, maybe that
        was the reason.

But it later became apparent that the small one was often pushed away
        from the food.
Those little critters had no manners; they were to their littlest companion,
        very rude.

There was a grossly overweight one, which may have been a mother-to-be
        in waiting.
With four raccoons in the garden, more on the way would be a disaster;
        about that there's no debating.

All of a sudden, out of the corner of her eye, she saw that another raccoon
        had joined the four.
That made Five, FIVE rambunctious raccoons just outside her door.
Madam Zucchini almost fell through the floor!
Surely this had to be the last addition; no matter how cute, she wanted there
        to be no more!

The first perplexing question in her mind was: Was this a family of five or a collection of relatives or a pack, OR?

The second question was: How did they all know to come for food at the patio door?

There must have been some system of communication for so many raccoons
         to be there.
One thing is for certain she said, "Out there is at least one very prolific pair."

The Gardener also caught by surprise asked, "Just what *are* their breeding and
         social habits?"
Shaking his head in amazement he said, "They must be breeders as active as
         mice and frisky rabbits."

Madam Zucchini decided she needed to research their habits to learn more.
She sighed deeply and said, "It's good for us to know exactly what more for us
         still could be in store."

He nodded in agreement and got up to watch as the five raccoons
         lumbered away.
He commented, "It would be neat to have a camera with a tracking device to
         follow them to see where they stay."

"Yes," Madam Zucchini agreed, "That would be great to find out.
That would clue us as to how large their territory is, which now is in doubt."

What is to be learned from this perplexing situation?

What more is in store for *The Garden of Surprises?*

With winter coming will the raccoons return in the spring?

The Night Marauder mystery was finally solved; but it took almost a
         year's time.
Thus ends the quest for **The Night Marauder** and The Gardener's story
         in rhyme.

The conclusion to this adventurous nature poem story is:

With land use development, our animal friends need help from time to time just to survive.
But, too much help will cause them to be too dependent when their own survival skills they need to revive.
Help them yes, but do not kill their will to forage for themselves to stay alive.
To remain independent is what each creature needs to do, to thrive.

We humans are the same; we need to take precautions that we on others do not totally rely;
It kills our human spirit to be beholden; it is to become dead before we die.

Work, Persistence and Patience in the end will finally get the reward.
But we must continue to persevere without becoming lax, lazy or bored.

Once we obtain one small goal, we must press on, and set others; we have to continue to work hard and believe.
Our lives will be easier with each and every step toward our life-time goals that we achieve.

What goals lead to success?

Success is achieving the goals WE set for ourselves, step by step.

The Garden of Surprises continues to surprise.

Madam Zucchini's book, *"The Mysterious Corncob Caper"* is a sequel to **The Night Marauder**. In it you will learn what other creatures visit **The Garden of Surprises** at night, sometimes even dining together with the raccoon family you met in this book. Available soon, order it on-line or at your favorite bookstore. You'll be surprised.

About the Writer/Illustrator

Doris Voss Dasenbrock, the author & illustrator of this publication holds a Bachelor's degree with a major in Art Education and a minor in English from the University of Wisconsin, Oshkosh. She holds an MFA degree from Florida State University. She majored in fine arts, drawing, and painting with a minor in the humanities.

She has taught art at all levels from elementary to high school, as well as night school adult classes in Wisconsin. In Florida, Maryland and Virginia she has taught college art classes. She also holds a marketing degree from the University of Maryland, University College, College Park.

She has traveled to many countries in Europe, Africa, Central, South, and North America, Asia and Pacific Islands. She has taken countless photos and currently writes, illustrates and paints. Her artwork has won numerous prizes and has been exhibited and purchased by both galleries and private collections nationally.

She has also worked commercially as a graphic artist, and as an advertising, marketing, and art director for a number of non-profit organizations and businesses located in the greater Washington, DC. Area.

www.ingramcontent.com/pod-product-compliance
Lightning Source LLC
Chambersburg PA
CBHW042117040426
42449CB00002B/73